Things we do in Timbuktu

by
Michael Lambert

Illustration by
Raymond P. Lambert III

Dedicated to our mother:

Sharion Gail Lambert

Things we do in Timbuktu

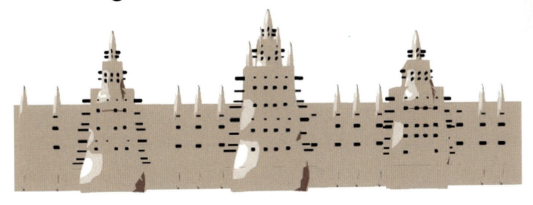

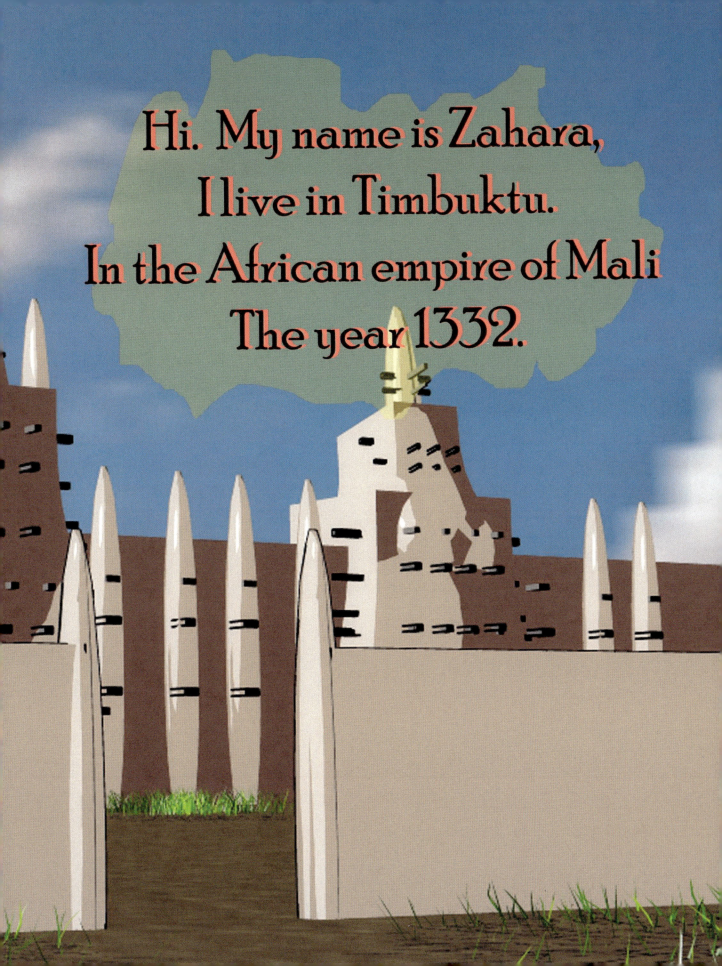

My father carries gold
In Saharan caravans.

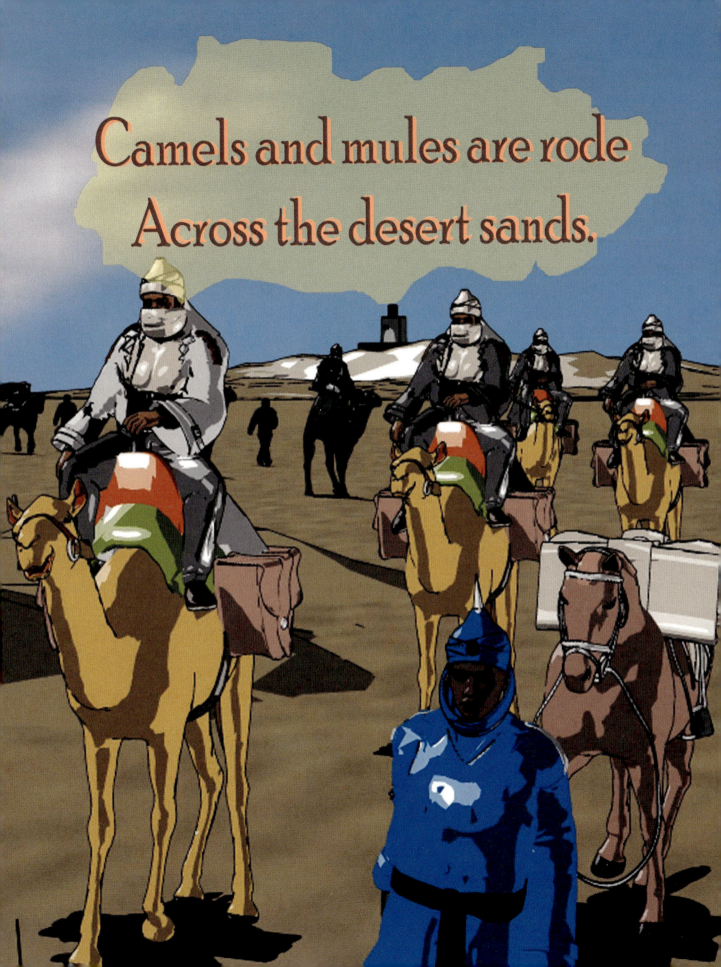

Down at our river Niger
My mother works as well.

Soldiers guard the city walls
To protect our heritage.

People fill our markets
They come from all around
They buy and sell, shop and trade
From sun up, to sun down.

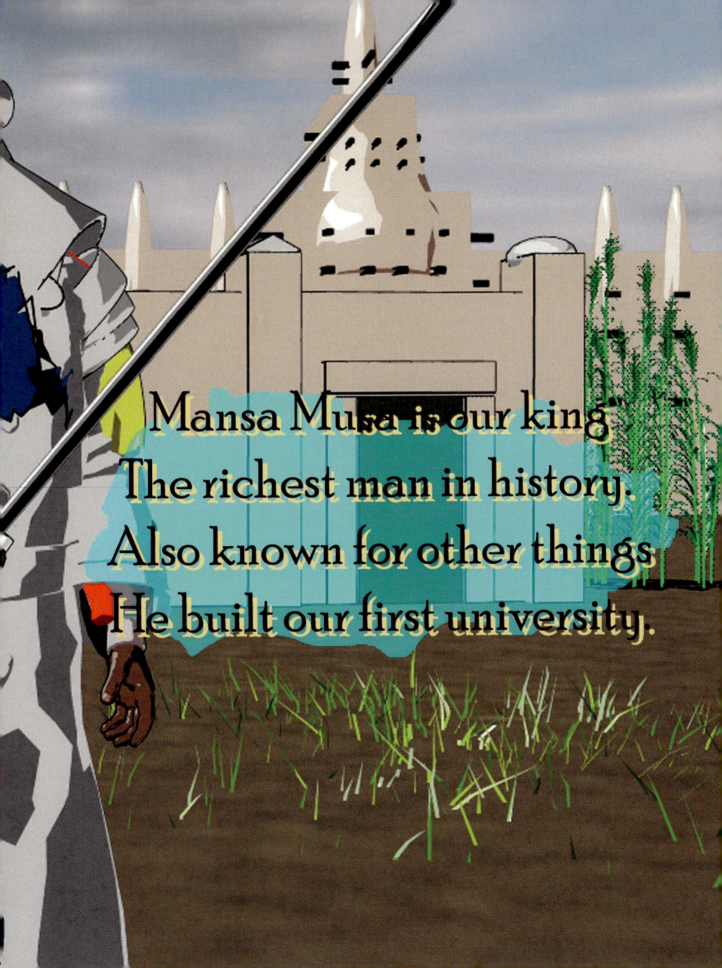

Mansa Musa is our king
The richest man in history.
Also known for other things
He built our first university.

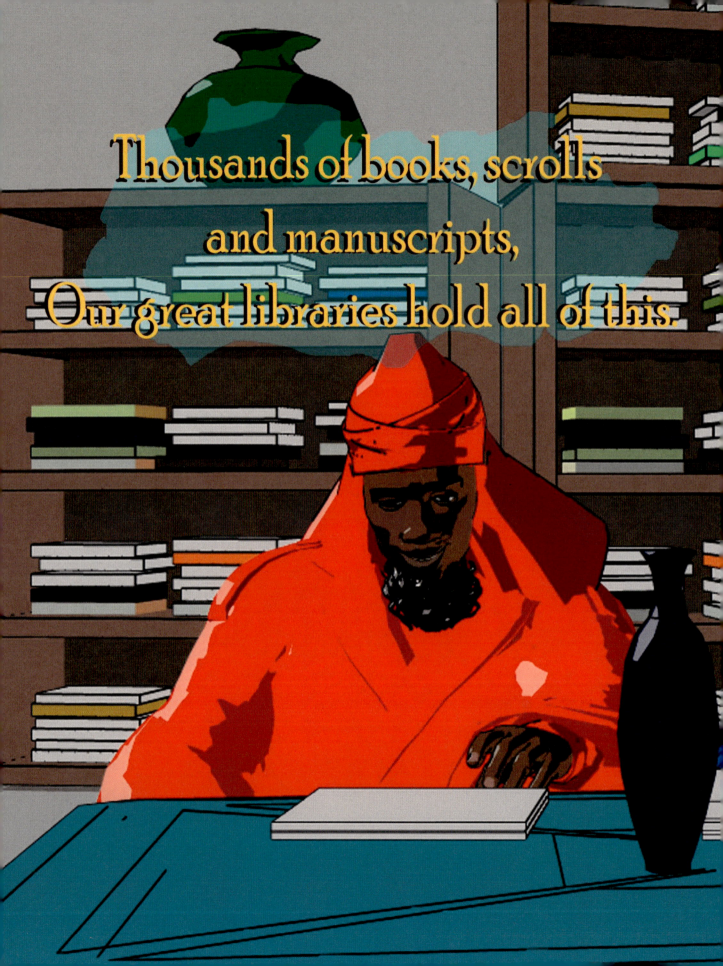

Thousands of books, scrolls
and manuscripts,
Our great libraries hold all of this.

Children care for our cattle and goats.
Feeding them fruits,
Wheat and sometimes oats.

We play games the rest of the day.
Hide and seek, tag, and keep away.

Elephants, hippos, lions, and gazelle.
Our plains, and rivers are
where they dwell.

Hot and sunny most times here.
Our rainy season last three months a year.

I hear my mother calling. That means it's time to eat.

So goodbye from Timbuktu.
Until next time we meet.

Ray and Michael Lambert's
first book "Black History Boy" is available
on Amazon.com. The Lambert Brothers
also write the Black History series "Black
History Boy" and "Black Archaeologist".
Both characters use a time machine
to visit great black people
and civilizations of the past.
Available at BlackArchaeologist.com

Made in United States
Orlando, FL
22 February 2022

15070731R00022